The Archbishop's School of Healing and Wholeness

Written by John W[...]

❦ ❦ ❦

Christian Healing starts [...]
and continues with us [...]

Section 1 **Before we go any further, let's define 'healing and wholeness'**

- Healing is a process rather than an isolated event; it is the journey into wholeness, freedom to be as God intends us to be.

- As human beings, we are all on that same journey; we are all in need of healing. It is, literally, the journey of a lifetime.

- We say we have been 'cured' when a particular problem has been sorted out e.g. a headache, a broken limb. Healing may include 'cure' but is about the bigger picture of body, mind and spirit – it is about the whole person.

- Healing is also about relationships which need to be in good order if we are to be whole and well. Healthy relationships are central to our wholeness.

- The Hebrew word *shalom* means much more than just 'peace'; it describes a state of affairs in which relationships are healthy, everyone has the resources they need for living and individuals in society work together in harmony for the common good.

- Whilst healing is about the individual, it is equally about families and communities, indeed about the whole of society.

Section 2 **What is 'Christian healing'?**

- Bishop Morris Maddocks once defined Christian healing as *Jesus Christ meeting you at the point of your need.*

- It is God's work of healing through Jesus Christ, a ministry of prayer and pastoral care entrusted to his Church. However, the Church does not have a monopoly – God heals through a great variety of channels.

- The Church's ministry is not in competition with the National Health Service (NHS); the Church sees medical professionals as partners in the work of caring and healing. Indeed, many Christians work within the NHS.

Section 3 Jesus brought healing and wholeness to those he met day by day:

- When we read the Gospels, we find Jesus concerned about the pain, disease and brokenness of people's lives.
- He brought the love and power of God to bear in every situation, changing lives in the process.
- He lived up to his name; 'Jesus' means 'deliverer', 'saviour' and is the Greek equivalent to 'Joshua' who led the Israelites to victory at Jericho.
- Almost every page of the four Gospels contains a story of healing. It is an artificial distinction to talk of 'Jesus' healing ministry' as against his 'teaching ministry'; his life and ministry were one and he responded to all requests for help in the appropriate way for that situation and individual. Whether teaching his disciples in the 'Sermon on the Mount' or restoring the centurion's servant to health, Jesus was bringing in God's kingdom of love.
- In the account of the healing of the ten lepers, Luke the physician and evangelist uses three different Greek words to describe what happened. These can be translated as 'cleansed', 'cured' and 'made whole'. The last implies 'salvation'. The man who returned to thank Jesus had truly started on the journey to wholeness, which included his relationship with God, through Jesus Christ (Luke 17: 11-19).

> *"Shalom – Soundness, Harmony, Adaptability, Love, Oneness, Movement"*
> (Howard Booth: *Health Healing & Wholeness*)

Section 4 Jesus commissioned his disciples to continue his mission:

We read in Luke 9 *Then Jesus called the twelve together and gave them power and authority over all demons and to cure diseases, and he sent them out to proclaim the kingdom of God and to heal.* Later on he sent out 70 others with the same commission. Sometime later *they returned with joy, saying "Lord, in your name even the demons submit to us!"* (Luke 10:17).

After the Resurrection of Jesus and the gift of the Holy Spirit at Pentecost, his apostles continued his healing work. For example, in Acts 3, Peter and John come across a lame man at the Beautiful Gate of the Temple. He was begging and was hoping for money, but Peter said to him:

"I have no silver or gold, but what I have I give you; in the name of Jesus Christ of Nazareth, stand up and walk." And he took him by the right hand and raised him up; and immediately his feet and ankles were made strong.

Section 5 *The healing ministry of the Church is being re-discovered today:*

- There was a revival of interest in the 20th century with the foundation of a number of healing institutions and agencies, including the Churches' Council for Health & Healing founded by William Temple in 1944.
- Churches of all denominations including Anglican, Roman Catholic, Methodist and URC have become involved.
- Whilst there is a place for the public rally with the well-known preacher, most of the time this ministry goes on quietly in the background without a lot of fuss or 'hype'.
- Resources for the healing ministry are freely available, in the form of specialist organisations and a wide range of literature (see *Resources*: page 12).
- The Anglican report *A Time to Heal* was published in 2000 as a result of a commission set up by the House of Bishops. Amongst its many recommendations are: 'parishes should ensure that the healing ministry is a part of normal everyday life, integrated into the wide range of activities already carried out, particularly pastoral care, and that it is made readily available to everyone including the unchurched.'
- The same report urges the Church to work alongside medical professionals, not in competition to them. Many years ago Bishop Morris Maddocks set up the Apostolate in which a local minister and a doctor agree to work together as a pair to put into practice this vision of collaboration.

Section 6 *What does all this mean in practice?*
The healing ministry has many facets:

- **Prayer** The ministry of healing prayer (James 5:16) brings those for whom we would pray into the presence of God. The four friends brought their paralysed friend to Jesus (Mark 2:1-12) – we do the same when we pray for someone who is ill or troubled. Church life should be characterised by prayer groups, prayer chains and praying individuals. This is a ministry in which all church members can participate.
- **Laying on of hands** This is found in Scripture for commissioning, blessing and healing. Jesus used it (e.g. Mark 1:41) and expected his disciples to do so (Mark 16:18). The sensitive use of touch can bring reassurance and a sense of belonging (see *Guidelines*: page 8).
- **Anointing** The disciples anointed with oil (Mark 6:13) as did congregations in the early church (James 5:14). In the Bible oil is connected with health and God's blessing. Used in healing, oil is sacramental – a visible sign of the work of God's Holy Spirit within the individual.

- **Ministry to the sick** The Church has always been involved in caring for those who are sick, whether at home or in hospital. Chaplains and visitors bring the love of Christ into these situations in a practical way. They help to keep sick people in touch with their local community.
- **Preaching the Gospel** We should regard healing as a natural consequence of preaching the Gospel (Acts 4:29-30). Healing is often the result of receiving the 'good news' (Gospel) of God's love for each one of us.
- **Reconciliation** The ministry of reconciliation (confession and absolution) brings the freedom of being forgiven (e.g. Mark 2:5-12). Forgiveness can be the gateway to healing and is central to the Christian 'good news'. We often emphasise the need to forgive others but forget the importance of forgiving ourselves.
- **Healing the family tree** Exploring the family tree can often highlight areas and relationships which need attention. In the celebration of the Holy Communion, earth and heaven are united in a unique way and any unfinished business with those who have died can be offered to God in prayer.
- **Healing of memories and emotional hurt** Many people are held back in their lives by the hurts and fears of the past. Prayer, anointing, confession and Holy Communion can bring release and healing in these areas.
- **Ministry to the dying** Those who are facing death, and their relatives, are in need of gentle pastoral care. By standing alongside, Christians can encourage them to realise that death is part of the healing process and that Christ has travelled that way before us; therefore we need not be afraid of the journey. The pastoral care of the bereaved is an important aspect of this ministry.
- **Deliverance** Sometimes healing prayer includes deliverance from oppression, evil and fear (Luke 9:1-2). This ministry should be practised only after careful training and preparation, and always by Christians working in a team. Most denominations have ministers who are authorised to assist local congregations when needed.
- **Relationships** There are four relationships which need to be right if we are to be whole and healthy – with God, with others, with ourselves and with our environment, planet Earth. Good loving Christian relationships should be rich in healing. Love drives out fear (1 John 4:18) which can be such a barrier to wholeness.
- **Worship** All worship – not only healing services – promotes healing. In particular, the Eucharist (Holy Communion) is itself the sacrament of healing. We are reminded of what Jesus has done for us upon the Cross for the forgiveness of sins and for our salvation (to save = to heal, rescue, make whole).
- **Listening** This is a ministry for us all if only we can put our own agendas to one side. Trained listeners (e.g. *Acorn Christian Listeners*) work in a

number of health centres – a good example of collaboration between Church and the health services. They are also to be found in cafes and drop-in centres in some of our towns and cities.

Section 7 **Practical steps in starting a healing ministry in your local church:**

- Organise a prayer partnership scheme e.g. prayer triplets or a prayer chain with telephone numbers.

- Have a prayer request board at the back of church or in a side chapel with request forms or cards. Decide when you will pray for those people, in private prayer and/or public worship.

- Invite members of the congregation to be intercessors i.e. to receive requests regularly.

- Invite house-bound members to make intercession their special ministry.

- Arrange regular prayer meetings ('Prayer for Healing').

- Publish a regular prayer letter with requests and helpful information, taking care to observe confidentiality where appropriate.

> **"** It soon became apparent that the profile of healing was more complex than I had first thought. It has become increasingly important to approach people not just as individuals but as individuals in community. In other words, we must take into account the past and present world of shaping circumstances that people bring with them when they come to the place of prayer. **"**
>
> (Russ Parker: *Healing Wounded History*)

- Offer the laying on of hands as part of a Eucharist, perhaps in a side chapel after receiving communion.

- Arrange an occasional healing service. This will require publicity, a liturgy, a number of ministers ('healing team'), a suitable location, prayer support, and most importantly the backing of the church council or equivalent body.

- Discuss the possibility of involving the congregation in the pastoral care/healing of the sick in their homes, perhaps in conjunction with home communion.

- Arrange an introductory course on the art of listening, perhaps with participants from other local churches as well as your own.

- In all these steps try to discover what is already happening in the other denominations in your area. Collaboration in the ministry of healing can be a great witness to the reconciling power of Christ.

- There are several good training courses available which can be used ecumenically e.g. *Growing a Healing Ministry* (Acorn), *Saints for Healing* (Lynx/SPCK), *Forward in Healing* (Grove Books).

Section 8 Guidelines for good practice:

- **Accountability** We are all accountable ultimately to God for the ministry of healing, whatever form it make take. Local prayer and healing teams must be accountable to the church leadership. Clear guidelines should be in place so that each member knows what is expected of them and knows where to turn for help and guidance.

- **Boundaries** Everyone involved must be aware of the necessity to respect personal and emotional boundaries. They should also be aware of their own limitations of training and experience and be able to refer people to others who can offer the skills that are needed.

- **Collaboration** The Church's healing ministry should be carried out in cooperation with health care officials and others in the local community. The approach should be 'both and' rather than 'either or'.

- **Competence** Preparation and training are important for this ministry and all involved should be on guard against conflicts of interest e.g. between the needs of the individual and those of the wider community.

- **Confidentiality** People's privacy and dignity should be respected at all times. A betrayal of confidence can have serious consequences and can lead to a lack of trust. Disclosure of personal details in public should be avoided e.g. on prayer boards. Whilst de-briefing is important in any team, confidentiality must always be maintained.

- **Consent** Those who are ministered to must give their consent and understand what is involved. Consent must never be taken for granted.

- **Counselling** Prayer for healing is sometimes confused with counselling. Counselling requires a trained counsellor and enough time in which to operate effectively.

- **Personal conduct** General manner and appearance is important. Team members must behave with courtesy and consideration. Personal hygiene is important, as is the balance between informality and intimacy.

- **Records** It is helpful to keep records of pastoral contacts. This should be done only with the individual's permission and confidentiality is vital.

- **Safety** All reasonable steps must be taken to ensure the safety of all involved. Physical arrangements should

> *" It has been said of medicine that its duty is sometimes to heal, often to afford relief, and always to bring consolation. This is exactly what the Bible tells us that God does for suffering humanity. Sometimes God heals, but not always. But He gives relief, He protects and sustains us in times of affliction; and His consolation is unending. Here too we may say that the doctor in his vocation works hand in hand with God. ""* (Dr Paul Tournier)

be carefully planned and there should be an awareness of situations to avoid.

- **Spiritual dangers** These include wanting to be a healer, doubting God's authority, being uncritical and blind to misuse, emphasising the powers of evil rather than the power of Christ, working alone rather than as a member of a team.

- **Supervision** Clergy and lay team members should be aware of the benefits of supervision. A regular opportunity to reflect on one's ministry is healthy for all concerned.

Section 9 *Frequently Asked Questions*

Does God send suffering?

No – God does not inflict suffering upon his children. The opposite is true – Jesus showed compassion for the sick and lost and accepted everyone who came to him for healing. It is God's will that we should be whole: *I came that they may have life and have it abundantly* (John 10:10).

The Old Testament emphasises the link between sin and suffering. However, when asked whose sin had caused the man to be born blind, Jesus clearly stated that his blindness was not a result of sin (John 9). We can, of course, cause suffering to others and to ourselves through our sins.

> *"Praise is inner health made audible "* (C.S. Lewis)

Does God use suffering?

Suffering can severely test our faith. 'Why has this happened to me?' we may ask. When we call out, 'My God, my God, why have you forsaken me' we echo the words of Jesus on the cross. He has been there before us and when we suffer he suffers too; he shares the pain and the anguish of our lives.

Yet through suffering we can grow and mature, knowing that Christ won the ultimate victory on Easter Day – the victory over sin and death. As St. Paul writes, *I consider that the sufferings of this present time are not worth comparing with the glory about to be revealed to us. We know that all things work together for good for those who love God* (Romans 8:18, 28). Sometimes this is seen in the life of a person who, whilst not healed from physical illness or limitation, is nevertheless a witness to the love and peace of God within.

Why are some people healed and not others?

When we pray for healing we should always be seeking God's will. No prayer is ever wasted, but the answer to our prayers may not be the one we are expecting. God hears and understands the cry from the heart when we pray

---

for a critically ill friend or relative and it would be wrong to suggest that we should not pray for a recovery to health in that situation. However, because we often concentrate on praying for physical cure we may not be expecting emotional and spiritual healing. Healing may involve coming to terms with physical illness and limitation.

I remember very clearly the evening when my sermon about healing was suddenly interrupted by a woman's cry, 'What about me?' Margaret was confined to a wheelchair and had been suffering from multiple sclerosis for some time. She and her friends had often prayed for her recovery, but with no obvious answer. She had come to the 'healing service' with those expectations, and was unable to contain her frustration and anger. Later in the service she did ask for prayer with the laying on of hands, and she died a short time afterwards. Her friends helped her discover God's peace before she died.

It is possible for healing to be blocked by emotional hurts, a lack of forgiveness or even by an unwillingness in the person concerned to be changed. The journey to wholeness necessarily involves change; sometimes we feel more secure as we are and afraid of change, even at the hands of God himself!

Should I throw away the pills and rely on prayer instead?

No. To stop taking medication prescribed by your doctor, or to opt out of medical or surgical treatment, would be irresponsible and reckless. God's healing comes through the proper use of professional medical skills. It is not 'either or' but 'both and'; continue to follow your doctor's advice and pray that through the treatment being offered you will be restored to health. Remember that there are many Christians working in all areas of the NHS and that you may well be in their prayers as they treat you in hospital, health centre or in your home.

Do certain people have the gift of healing and how do I know if I have the gift?

All Christians are called and empowered to pray for others; we do that in our own private prayers, with others in church or chapel and sometimes when we are sitting alongside the person who is ill. The Church's ministry of healing should involve all of God's people.

God does give gifts of healing to individuals for use within the fellowship of the Church; St. Paul includes these in his list of spiritual gifts in 1 Corinthians 12. Down the centuries there have been people who have used such a gift to bring healing and wholeness to others. Dorothy Kerin, the founder of Burrswood, a multi-disciplinary Christian healing centre in Kent, comes to mind; she was obedient to God's call and unselfishly exercised a wide-ranging healing ministry.

I remember the words of a colleague some years ago when I introduced the healing ministry into the life of the cathedral community where I worked. He said, 'I am not against it, but I don't have the gift of healing'. I tried to point out to him that all members of the body of Christ have a healing ministry, but he still felt unable to be involved.

The local church or chaplaincy community is the context in which gifts of healing should be recognised and used.

> " *Are any among you suffering? They should pray. Are any cheerful? They should sing songs of praise. Are any among you sick? They should call for the elders of the church and have them pray over them, anointing them with oil in the name of the Lord. The prayer of faith will save the sick.* "
> (James 5:13-15a)

Teamwork is important and offers the possibility of testing out perceived gifts of healing.

What is the Christian attitude to complementary and alternative therapies?

First we need to distinguish between the two terms. *Complementary* means 'in support of conventional medicine'; *alternative* means 'instead of conventional medicine'.

Sadly there has been quite a lot of 'hot air' talked in some Christian circles about these modern therapies. Sometimes they have been condemned out of hand as 'of the devil'.

Many therapies such as acupuncture and reflexology have come to us from the East where they have been recognised for thousands of years as effective and safe. Increasingly, Western medicine is regarding such treatments as truly 'complementary'.

How can the Christian distinguish between all these different treatments? I would suggest four important steps:

1. Find out the facts about the therapy, its history and methods. The chapter 'Complementary Medicine and Alternative Approaches' in the report *A Time to Heal* is a good starting point. Dr Gareth Tuckwell and the Revd David Flagg also deal with this area in their book *A Question of Healing* (see *Further Reading*: page 12).

2. Check the integrity of its practitioners, both locally and through a national body if one exists.

3. Bring all that into your prayers to allow the Holy Spirit's discernment to guide you and any decision you will make.

4. Share your findings with fellow Christians within the fellowship of your local church.

Paul writes to the Thessalonians, *Do not quench the Spirit … but test everything; hold fast to what is good; abstain from every form of evil.* (1 Thessalonians 5:19-22) I have personal experience of both Reiki and the Alexander Technique. Reiki means 'universal life force energy' and has its origins in ancient Buddhism; Alexander discovered how to re-educate the body to avoid the common misuse of the spine and neck. Both are concerned with the whole person and with balance and well-being. Each has found a place in my ministry alongside my prayers, as part of God's rich tapestry of wholeness.

What should be my expectations when I pray for healing, either for myself or for others?

I believe strongly that no prayer is ever wasted. This means that whether I pray with great expectations or with little faith, the very act of communicating with our loving heavenly Father helps to bring about more of what he wills for his children. The key point here is surely that it must be 'Thy will, not mine, be done'. If we try to tell God what to do or how he should answer our prayers we may well feel disappointed. Conversely, if we pray that the outcome will be according to God's will and purpose we will often be surprised by the 'answer'.

We all pray with expectations and if we are not careful we can raise false expectations. What do I mean by that? Simply that the person for whom we are praying will expect God to act in a certain way because of how we have prayed. If God does not, they might feel let down or even that their faith is not great enough. That would be a negative and even harmful outcome to prayer.

I will always remember the practice at the regular healing services at Burrswood. I was privileged to spend a month there as an assistant chaplain in 1995. Staff members would minister in pairs to those asking for prayer. The words they used were striking: that the person would become as God wanted them to be, according to his loving purposes for their lives. I never felt that that kind of prayer was avoiding responsibility; rather it was an enabling kind of prayer.

What is the place of faith in praying for healing?

In many of the healing stories in the Gospels, Jesus looked for faith in God in the lives of those involved. To the woman healed at the moment when she touched his robe in the crowded street, Jesus said, *Daughter, your faith has made you well; go in peace* (Luke 8:48).

Mark describes how the four friends let their paralysed friend through the roof; it was when Jesus 'saw their faith' that he forgave and restored their friend (Mark 2: 1-12).

Sometimes when we pray for the sick we feel desperate, as if prayer is the last resort. Yet even in that situation we are exercising faith in a loving God who we believe can help. It was Corrie ten Boom who said that it is not the size of your faith that matters; rather that you have faith in a great God. Jesus spoke of 'faith the size of a mustard seed' being able to achieve great things, even the moving of mountains!

On occasion, faith may follow healing rather than precede it. I think this happened in the case of the leprosy sufferer who returned to thank Jesus (see *Section 3*: page 2).

> **"** *Do not try to manipulate God in the guise of having faith in him. Faith is not getting God to give his attention to what we are focusing on, but giving our attention to what he is focusing on.* **"**
>
> (John Richards: *Faith & Healing*)

Does the Cross have healing powers?

Yes, but we have to beware of being sentimental or superstitious when thinking of the Cross. At our baptism we are signed with the sign of the Cross, the Christian badge. It is a symbol of God's healing and forgiving love at work in that individual's life. Yet we so easily take the cross for granted because we see it everywhere. Ornate crosses are found both in churches and in the jeweller's window – far removed from the rough wooden cross of Good Friday.

I have a 'holding cross' made of olive wood from Bethlehem. It is usually in my pocket and I find myself holding it much of the time, almost without realising it. Yes, it is reassuring but not in any superstitious kind of way. There is no magic in such a cross; rather it is a reminder that the battle against sin and death is already won through the death and resurrection of Christ.

Some years ago now, on a Sunday morning in between services, I was asked to see two young men who were rather disturbed. I listened to their story and prayed with them before they left to drive back home, a journey of several miles. I later heard from one of them how on the journey back that morning he had felt a weight across his shoulders and back in the shape of a cross. It persisted through that evening but for the first time for many months he slept well. When he awoke he knew he was different; he was free from the past and its addictions and was hopeful for the future. The cross he felt was a sign of deliverance and healing – of the Spirit of God at work in his life in the name of Christ.

Can children be involved in the ministry of healing?

Yes, they most certainly can. I have known children to minister healing prayer to adults; they have a simplicity and directness in prayer which is refreshing and their dynamic faith often puts adults to shame! Within a Christian family it is natural for children to pray for their parents, and vice versa.

We must, however, be aware of the importance of child protection in this as in all areas of ministry.

Section 10 *Resources:*

(a) FURTHER READING

A Time to Heal: A report for the House of Bishops on the Healing Ministry (Church House Publishing, 2000)

Banks, John; *The Leaves of the Tree* (Moorley's, 2002)

Booth, Howard; *Health, Healing & Wholeness* (Arthur James, 1998)

Cowie, Ian; *Jesus' Healing Works and Ours* (Wild Goose Publications, 2000)

Lawrence, Roy; *How to Pray when Life Hurts* (Scripture Union, 1993)

Maddocks, Morris; *The Christian Healing Ministry* (SPCK 1990)

Mitton, Michael; *Wild Beasts & Angels* (DLT, 2000)

Parker, Russ; *Healing Wounded History* (DLT, 2001)

Stanley, Simon; *The Archbishop's School of the Sacraments* (York Courses, 2002)

Tuckwell, Gareth & Flagg, David; *A Question of Healing* (Eagle, 2000)

Twycross, R. et al; *Mud and Stars* (Sobell Publications, Oxford, 1991)

(b) SOME HEALING ORGANISATIONS

Acorn Christian Foundation, Whitehill Chase, High Street, Bordon, Hants, GU35 0AP. *Resourcing and encouraging the Christian Healing Ministry, Christian Listeners and collaboration with medicine.* Tel. 01420 478121.

Burrswood Christian Centre, Groombridge, Tunbridge Wells, Kent, TN3 9PY. *A multi-disciplinary community offering hospital care, physiotherapy, counselling, hydrotherapy and pastoral care.* Tel. 01892 863637.

Centre for Health and Pastoral Care, Holy Rood House with Thorpe House, 10 Sowerby Road, Sowerby, Thirsk, YO7 1HX. *Residential therapeutic centre for spiritual direction, Christian healing, professional counselling and pastoral care.* Tel. 01845 522580.

Crowhurst Christian Healing Centre, The Old Rectory, Crowhurst, Battle, East Sussex, TN33 9AD. (The Divine Healing Mission) *A residential centre offering the healing touch of Christ through worship and healing prayer. Also runs training courses.* Tel. 01424 830204.

Guild of Health, PO Box 227, Epsom, KT19 9WQ. *Helping people to experience freedom and life through prayer and sacraments within the fellowship of God's family.* Tel. 020 8786 0517.

Guild of St. Raphael, 2 Green Lane, Tuebrook, Liverpool, L13 7EA. *Encourages a sacramental approach to wholeness in Christ through its local branches and affiliated churches.* Tel. 0151 228 3193.